Third Edition

Apple Country Cooking

Apple Recipes, Anecdotes,
and a
Commemoration of Johnny Appleseed

Patricia B. Mitchell

Copyright © 1989, 1990, 1991 by Patricia B. Mitchell. All rights reserved.

Published 1991 by the author.
Mail: Mitchells, Box 429, Chatham, VA 24531
    Book Sales: 800-967-2867
    E-mail: *Answers@FoodHistory.com*
    Websites: *FoodHistory.com* and *MitchellsPublications.com*

Compact Edition
Printed in the U.S.A.
ISBN-10: 0-925117-47-1
ISBN-13: 978-0-925117-47-2

Thirteenth Printing, April 2013

– *Illustrations* –

Front cover – "A-peelin'" by Henry H. Mitchell.

Inside title page – "Johnny's Contemplation" by Henry H. Mitchell.

Page 37 – Adapted from "Blossom and Fruit Design," *Peterson's Magazine*, July 1887.

Rear cover – "Autumn," from the cover of *Godey's Lady's Book*, vol. 65, November 1862.

Graphic research and design are by Sarah E. Mitchell, *VintageDesigns.com*.

Table of Contents

Seeds of a New Nation 1
Classic Waldorf Salad 2
Finger-Lickin' Apple Butter Ribs 3
Old Germantown Omelet 4
"Westward, Ho!" Meat Loaf 5
Pan-Fried Pork Chops with Apples 6
Mom's Fried Apples 8
Creole Apple Jelly 9
Picayune Apple Sauce 9
Old-Timey Indoor Apple Butter 10
Current (Up-to-Date) Apple Butter 11
Sought-After Apple Butter Bread 11
Exciting News Apple Butter Muffins 12
Epps's Apple-Banana-Bran Muffins 13
Applesauce Pancakes 14
Gift-Quality Apple Butter Nut Bread 14
Flag-Flying Birthday Cake 15
Margot's Apple Strudel 16
Newlywed Apple Cake 17
Butterscotch Applesauce Cake 18
Make-Somebody-Happy Applesauce Cake 19
Caramel Frosting 20
Country Kitchen Apple Cake 21
Old Virginia Applesauce Cake 21
Eureka Apple Butter Cake 22
Dried Apple Pies 24
Dried Apple Cake 24
Midwest Apple Pie Cake 25
Mama's Apple Pie 26
Unsurpassed Pie Pastry 26
Crazy Crust Apple Pie 27
Whispering Pines Fruit Kuchen 28
Applestreuselkuchen 29
Dutch Apple Pie 30
Apple Johnny-Cake 32
Apple-Pear Pie 32
Pioneer Pumpkin – Apple Butter Pie 33
Applesauce Pies 34
Heirloom Apple Fritters 34
Extraordinarily Good Apple Butter Bars 35
Winter Thaw Hot Cider 36
On-the-Wagon Champagne 37

Seeds of a New Nation

John Chapman ("Johnny Appleseed"), pioneer/preacher/nurseryman extraordinaire, contributed more to the well-being and beauty of our nation than did many of the more highly-touted patriots, politicians, and philanthropists. Behind the whimsical, almost mythological mental image we have of the eccentric fellow clad in a coffee sack and pot-for-a-hat, stands a real man who gave unselfishly of himself and his resources — apple seeds and sprouts — to further the propitious development of this country. Johnny Appleseed's deeds will be more deeply explored in this volume, and I will also include numerous personal apple-related recollections and recipes.

John Chapman was born around 1774 in Leominster, Massachusetts, and lived until 1843, at which time his body was found, true to character, lying in an apple orchard near Fort Wayne, Indiana. In his lifetime, this botanist/herb doctor had endeared himself to thousands of pioneer families, Native Americans, and animals.

He dearly loved Jesus (although his Swedenborgian theology was definitely not in the Christian mainstream), God's creations, and "little green (or red or yellow) apples." In fact, his favorite foods were said to have been buttermilk, beebread (the pollen substance in honeycombs upon which bees feed), and Rambo apples. Living as he did, often out-of-doors, sleeping in logs and cooking over a campfire, we can easily speculate that he consumed many of his beloved apples in their natural state — fresh and raw, that is. Perhaps sometimes he fried them, and, of course, when he was invited to dine in a settler's cabin, presumably the woman prepared cooked apple treats for him — baked apples, Apple Betty, apple pie, etc. However, the opening recipe in this compendium will demonstrate the use of uncooked apples.

Classic Waldorf Salad

Not a lot of foods can claim to have been "invented" in the United States. A few do qualify, though. Peanut butter, potato chips, hamburgers, chow mein, chop suey, and Waldorf Salad are American ideas!

I have enjoyed this kind of salad ever since I learned to chew. Light and refreshing, with the surprising burst of flavor of walnuts (or the more subtle taste of pecans), this salad will be remembered by you, too, as a favorite.

$1/2$ c. mayonnaise (or less if desired)
2 tbsp. lemon juice
2 c. red apples, unpeeled, cored, and diced
1 c. celery, thinly sliced
$1/2$ c. walnuts, chopped (or pecans, if preferred)
$1/2$ c. dark seedless raisins
$1/4$ - $1/2$ tsp. ginger (optional)

In a medium-sized bowl, mix the mayonnaise with the lemon juice. Stir in the remaining ingredients. Toss gently. Chill. Serve on lettuce leaves. Yield: 4 servings.

Notes: Diced red apples can also be added to coleslaw, potato salad, and tuna salad. Innovative, hey?! — And very pretty to look at!

Perhaps you will choose a McIntosh from Wisconsin or a Winesap from Virginia for use in a salad. Other recommended varieties for salads include Delicious, Jonathan, Courtland, York Imperial, Baldwin, Gravenstein, and Yellow Newtown.

One of the most pleasing characteristics of apples is their versatility. Among the seven kinds of wild apple trees that are found in the United States, and the many commercially-

developed varieties, there is an apple flavor and texture to suit every taste, whether for eating raw or cooking. Apples, like tomatoes, are to me among the indispensable adjuncts of good cooking. The next few recipes show how apples can appear as the "star" of the meal — in the main course.

Finger-Lickin' Apple Butter Ribs

I think of barbecued ribs as a basic, back-to-nature fun food. Especially when you eat them with your hands (is it actually possible to partake of them any other way?), they seem deliciously primitive. Perhaps Johnny Appleseed's friends, the Shawnee Indians (who had made the peculiar, rugged white man an honorary member of their tribe because of his knowledge of herbs, his seeming ability to communicate with animals, his courage, and his overall familiarity with folkways) cooked deer meat in this fashion (though Chapman himself was a vegetarian): venison ribs with a flavorful sauce of wild berries, herbs, and, who knows, maybe even a few apples thrown in!

4 or 5 pork ribs
Salt, black pepper, and (*lots* of) garlic powder
¼ c. water
1 (10.5 oz.) can tomato soup
1 c. apple butter
¼ c. vinegar (apple cider vinegar *or* white vinegar)
¼ c. onion, chopped
¼ c. celery, chopped (optional)
¼ c. green pepper, chopped
1 tsp. liquid smoke
1 tsp. ginger root, chopped, *or* a dash of ground ginger

Place ribs in a roasting pan. Sprinkle generously with salt, pepper, and garlic powder. Steam over charcoal (or in a 375° F. oven) for 45 minutes. Meanwhile, combine the remaining ingredients in a saucepan, heat, and simmer 45 minutes. Remove the ribs from roasting pan to a grill over hot charcoal. Baste with sauce. Cook ribs, basting frequently, for 30 minutes or until done (turn them about every 10 minutes). Serve with extra sauce.

Old Germantown Omelet

The next recipe may be served as a side dish with pork or ham, or as a dessert.

❧❧❧❧❧❧❧

4 large apples, peeled, cored, and sliced
2 tbsp. water
2 tbsp. butter
6 tbsp. sugar
1 tsp. grated lemon peel
1 tbsp. lemon juice
1 egg, well beaten
1 c. coarse bread crumbs
1 tbsp. sugar (optional)

Cook apples with water in covered saucepan over low heat, stirring occasionally. When apples are soft, stir in butter and sugar. Cool slightly; stir in lemon peel, lemon juice, and beaten egg. Butter a 1-quart casserole dish and sprinkle $\frac{1}{2}$ c. crumbs in bottom; pour in apple mixture and sprinkle remaining crumbs and sugar on top. Bake at 350° F. for $\frac{1}{2}$ hour. Yield: 6 servings.

Note: This recipe, originally entitled "Friar's Omelet," is from *The Clivedon Recipe Book*, Cliveden (the "Chew House"), Philadelphia, Pennsylvania.

Johnny Appleseed's labors are still evident in a 100,000-square-mile area of Ohio and Indiana. Although he was born near Boston, Massachusetts, he moved as a young man to Fort Duquesne, Pennsylvania (now known as Pittsburgh) and bought a small farm. By this time he had already discovered that he had a knack for growing fruit trees, so, of course, he planted an orchard.

Although Pittsburgh was considered "west" at that time in history, pioneers pressing farther west toward the wilderness of the Ohio Valley traveled past Johnny's farm almost constantly (he often provided them with free food and lodging). Johnny felt that these people would surely miss the beauty of expansive apple orchards in the Spring — their blossoms a billowing wave of white and pink petals. He knew that they would miss harvesting juicy sweet apples, so, he decided to do what he could to help. He began his project by collecting the residue from cider presses in western Pennsylvania. He spent endless hours picking the apple seeds out of the sticky mash, then drying the seeds, and finally filling little hand-sewn deerskin bags with the precious germs of life. To westward-bound passers-by he gave some fresh apples from his apple storage cave and a pouch of seeds (which, in effect, was giving them a potential orchard).

The next recipe contains no apple seeds, hopefully, but the surprise of apples, nutmeg, and cubed cheese in a meat loaf. These ingredients give an unusual but welcome twist to a conventional dish.

"Westward, Ho!" Meat Loaf

2 lb. ground beef
1 c. applesauce
1 tsp. salt (or less, to suit taste)
$1/2$ tsp. nutmeg (or less, to suit taste)
$1/4$ tsp. black pepper (or less, to suit taste)
$1 1/2$ c. soft bread crumbs
1 medium onion, chopped
1 egg, beaten
4 oz. Cheddar cheese, cut into approximately 20 cubes

Mix all ingredients. Transfer into a 9x5-inch loaf pan and bake at 350° F. for 1 hour and 15 minutes. Remove from oven and let sit for 10 minutes before taking out of the pan. Serves 8 or more.

By and by, wanderlust struck Johnny. He realized that his seeds and seedlings would need attention out west — someone who knew how to plant and care for the little trees. So, the orchardman gave his Pennsylvania farm to a widow with a large needy family, bought two Indian canoes, and lashed them together. He loaded them with apple seeds and then drifted down the Ohio River. He did not buy a farm, but instead lived the life of something of a vagabond, planting and then tending nurseries throughout Ohio. Sometimes he returned East to get more throwaway seeds from the Pennsylvania cider presses. Always planting, and giving away (or selling for next to nothing, or swapping for old clothes) the seeds and seedlings, it is certainly possible that John Chapman was responsible for the existence of hundreds of thousands of apple trees. Perhaps when you chop the apples for the following Pan Fried Pork Chops, you will, as I do, visualize the individualistic chap sitting beside his campfire, cooking cornmeal mush in his pot/pan/kettle hat, and reflectively chewing on an apple.

Pan-Fried Pork Chops with Apples

2 tbsp. all-purpose flour
$1/4$ tsp. salt
$1/8$ tsp. black pepper
4 pork chops
Butter *or* margarine
2 apples, cut in wedges
$1/4$ c. orange juice
$1/4$ c. raisins
$1/4$ tsp. cinnamon (or less, to suit your taste)

Combine flour, salt, and black pepper in a small paper bag. Drop pork chops into the bag, one at a time, and shake to coat.

Meanwhile, melt the butter in a skillet. Add meat and brown. Add remaining ingredients; simmer, covered, until chops (and apples) are done. Serve meat smothered in apples and pan drippings. Serves 4.

Commercially speaking, the state of Washington is "apple country," because it leads in apple production. (Washington apple production began in Fort Vancouver in 1827 and now half of all fresh apples sold in America are grown there, with more than 4,500 apple growers producing 7 billion apples annually.) Other big producers include California, Maine, Massachusetts, Michigan, New Jersey, New York, North Carolina, Ohio, Pennsylvania, Virginia, and West Virginia.

From a historical perspective, the New England states, Virginia, and the Ohio Valley could be called "apple country." From a practical culinary viewpoint, Tennessee to Texas, Arkansas to Alaska, and 'most everywhere in between is "apple country," for what cook in town or country does not take pride in preparing apples (those sweetly edible members of the rose family) in numerous ways to please the palates of family and friends?!

We had six good-sized apple trees in our yard in Dry Fork, Virginia, where I grew up. Three of the trees produced fair Yellow Transparent apples. The others produced (grudgingly) some rather nondescript red apples. All the apples were small, oft-misshapen, really suitable more for cooking than eating out of hand. Yet, despite the somewhat mediocre fruit, those trees "earned their keep." One of the trees was a particular favorite of the birds, every season housing several nests in its branches. (We also hung two birdhouses on its limbs, and they both were always occupied.) This same tree supported a rope and plank swing for me. A metal swing set sat under the shade of another apple tree.

My favorite apple tree, however, was one which grew behind our garage. Beneath this tree was our grape arbor. I loved to climb up the tree and step over to the sloping garage roof. Once on the roof, I could pick an apple; and, because the grapevine had used the apple tree as a trellis, I could gather a handful of "fox" grapes or purple grapes. With my snack in hand, I'd sit on the roof, open a book (which I usually brought up) and while away a pleasant afternoon until Mom called.

Mom's Fried Apples

12 good-sized cooking apples, quartered
$1/2$ c. water
$1/4$ to $1/2$ c. sugar (depending upon the sweetness of the fresh apples, and upon how sweet you want the finished product to be)
$1/2$ stick ($1/4$ c.) margarine (You can, of course use butter. Mom and I happen to prefer margarine. If you want to live "high on the hog," use bacon drippings!)

Put the apples in a skillet with the water. (You needn't peel the apples.) Cover and simmer until tender (20 - 30 minutes), stirring occasionally. When the apples are soft, add the sugar and margarine. Heat and serve.

My husband and I lived in New Orleans for about four years. I don't have to tell you about the wonderful food there — Creole and Cajun cuisines have rightfully earned their reputations as being incomparable, but I will tell you an "apple memory" associated with New Orleans. While there, we did not eat breakfast at Brennan's, lunch at Galatoire's, and dinner at Antoine's every day! Actually, most days around noon you would find us in our retail gift shop hurriedly wolfing down a peanut butter or cheese sandwich and an apple. (Incidentally, the apples I was able to purchase at the French Quarter grocery store near us did in no way measure up to the quality of apples available in Virginia.) Anyway, an old gentleman friend of ours often stopped in to "chew the fat" with us at lunchtime. I will always remember the rather off-putting taste of peanut butter eaten while breathing in aromatic Havana (!) cigar smoke! (Somehow, an apple eaten amid wafting cigar fumes was not nearly as repulsive as that rich peanut butter!) Strangely, I still adore peanut butter sandwiches, and I think I could **live** off **apples**.

By the way, here are two apple recipes from the second edition (1901) of **The Picayune's Creole Cook Book**, published by the New Orleans daily newspaper, **The Picayune**.

Creole Apple Jelly

1 lb. of sugar to every pint of juice

Take pippins or other tart apples, pare them and cut into quarters, put into a preserving kettle, cover with water, add the grated rind of a lemon and let them boil to a marmalade. Then strain the juice, without squeezing, through a clean jelly bag made of flannel, and for every pint of juice add one pound of fine sugar. If the apples are not very tart, add the juice also.

Picayune Apple Sauce

6 large apples
2 tbsp. butter
4 cloves
1 stick cinnamon
1 c. water

Cut the apples into pieces, peel, and let them boil till mashed into a jelly, stirring frequently, to prevent burning. Add the ground cloves and the stick of cinnamon, ground fine. Let them boil at least three-quarters of an hour, mashing as they become tender. Then take off the fire, and press them through a coarse sieve. Add sugar to taste, add the butter, and set all back on the fire, and let it simmer gently for five minutes longer. Set to cool in a dish, and serve with Roast Pork or Roast Goose. The sauce must not scorch, or the taste will be spoiled.

It is likely that apple butter was part of John Chapman's motivation for distributing his seeds and seedlings. I suspect that besides enjoying the taste of the luscious spread, he realized the value of the social customs associated with the preparation of apple butter, and not wanting people to be deprived of either the condiment itself or its "group activity" method of production, he determined to extend the number of apple orchards westward as the pioneers pushed in that direction.

Apple butter is called "lottwaerrick" in Pennsylvania Dutch dialect. It is defined as a kind of jam made with apples stewed with spices. The procedure of making apple butter by boiling the fruit over an outdoor fire was a technique brought to this country from the German Palatinate region (where apples and other fruits were slowly cooked in this manner). To make lottwaerrick required many hands to cut the apple slices ("schnitz"), and to stir the kettle. Often young couples got together for "schnitzing," stirring, and sighing (as they gazed soulfully into each other's eyes!). — Another word to add to your Pennsylvania Dutch vocabulary is "feinschmeckers," which is one way this Germanic group describes themselves. It means "those who know how good food should taste."

Old-Timey Indoor Apple Butter

8 qt. sweet cooking apples, unpeeled, cored, cut into eighths
(Some old-timers in these parts used Pippins or Summer Rambos, but the modern varieties will work fine, too.)
1 qt. apple cider
1 qt. water
10 c. sugar

2 tsp. cinnamon
½ tsp. cloves
½ tsp. allspice (optional)

In a large pot, cook the apples, cider, and water until the apples are soft. Press through a strainer. Put into a big kettle or two roasters (whichever will fit into your oven). Stir in half of the sugar. Bake at 350° F., stirring every half hour with a wooden spoon. After one hour of cooking, add the remaining 5 cups of sugar and the spices. Cook until the apple butter is thick and deep brownish red. This will probably take 3 more hours. Remember to stir every half hour. When cooked, pour into sterilized jars and seal.

Current (Up-to-Date) Apple Butter

1 (64-oz.) jar unsweetened applesauce, warmed
1 tsp. cinnamon
1 c. sugar

Pour hot applesauce into a roaster. Add sugar and cinnamon, and stir well. Bake at 200° F. - 225° F. for 8 hours. Pour into sterilized jars and seal.

Sought-After Apple Butter Bread

One morning as I was lying in bed, waiting for it to be time to get up, the basic idea for this bread recipe came into my mind. However, that first inspiration involved stirring the apple butter in last to create a swirly, "marbleized" pattern of dark, reddish-brown apple butter in the baked slices of bread. For some reason that idea didn't "pan out" — no apple butter streaks were evident. (I guess it was diffused throughout the loaf.) But the recipe is good anyway!

੨੦੨੦੨੦੨੦੨੦੨੦

1½ c. unbleached *or* all-purpose flour
1 c. whole wheat flour
2 tsp. baking powder
¼ tsp. salt
¼ c. sugar
½ c. pecans *or* other nuts, chopped
2 tbsp. vegetable oil
1 c. milk
¾ c. apple butter

    Combine the dry ingredients. In another bowl, mix the last three ingredients. Combine the two mixtures, and spoon into a greased 9x5-inch loaf pan. Bake at 350° F. for 50 minutes or until done.

Note: You may substitute apple butter in bread or cake recipes which call for applesauce and cinnamon and other "apple pie" type spices: cloves, allspice, nutmeg. Just use an equal amount of apple butter in place of the applesauce, and omit the spices.

Exciting News Apple Butter Muffins

    My family and I enjoy these "gems" at breakfast time, and we, like folks everywhere, enjoy stimulating conversation with a meal. Wouldn't it have been fun to have invited Mr. Appleseed to dine and spend the night, as many of the settlers did? Imagine hearing his news from the pioneers, the Indians, and his "news fresh from Heaven," as he called his preaching and reading of Scripture. But actually, with reference to our imaginary story about Mr. Appleseed's spending the night, he would probably have politely declined the offer. He preferred to sleep outside with animal friends!

1 egg
1 c. milk
1 c. all-purpose flour
1 c. whole wheat flour

4 tsp. baking powder
¾ tsp. salt
2 tbsp. brown sugar
1 c. raisins
2 tbsp. butter *or* margarine, melted
½ c. apple butter

    Beat together the egg and milk. In a separate container, mix the dry ingredients. Combine these two mixtures. Blend in the melted butter and apple butter last. Spoon into 12 greased muffin cups and bake at 400° F. for around 20 minutes.

    The next two recipes come from the kitchen of my artist friend Epps Perrow of Hurt, Virginia. She is a lady who uses both paints and pots with remarkable skill.

Epps's Apple-Banana-Bran Muffins

1 c. All-Bran cereal
1 c. milk

1¼ c. all-purpose flour
1 tbsp. baking powder
¼ tsp. salt
2 tsp. sugar (*or* one packet Sweet 'n' Low)

1 banana, mashed
1 apple, chopped
1 egg, beaten
3 tbsp. vegetable oil

    Soak together the All-Bran cereal and milk. Meanwhile mix the dry ingredients. In another bowl combine the last four ingredients. Next mix everything together, and spoon into 12 greased and heated muffin tins. Bake at 400° F. for about 20 minutes.

Applesauce Pancakes

1 c. all-purpose flour
2 tsp. baking powder
1 tsp. salt
4 eggs, well-beaten
1 #2 can (20 oz. or 2 ½ c.) applesauce
¼ c. butter, melted

Sift dry ingredients. Add to beaten eggs, applesauce, and butter mixture, and proceed as in preparing ordinary pancakes.

Gift-Quality Apple Butter Nut Bread

Besides his Swedenborgian theology and eloquent Bible reading, his information about other settlers, and stories about the Native Americans, Johnny Appleseed was a "sight for sore eyes" to the lonely pioneer because he came bearing gifts. As you might suspect, he had saplings and herbs for Pa and Ma. He also saved up interesting rocks and shells for the lads, and bits of calico for the lassies.

This saintly human never harmed man or beast, going so far as to extinguish his campfire rather than allow gnats to be burned in the flames. In the fall of the year, he would round up abandoned, decrepit horses, and feed and care for them until spring, using profits from tree sales to buy their food. — He carried no weapons. He played with bear cubs in sight of their mother, and kept a pet wolf which he had nursed back to health after freeing it from a trap. To just begin to emulate Chapman's generous, open nature, become a giver and bake these loaves to share!

3 ½ c. whole wheat flour
2 tsp. baking soda
2 ½ tsp. nutmeg

2 tsp. cinnamon
²/₃ c. sugar
¹/₃ c. vegetable oil
2 eggs
2¼ c. milk (this amount may need to be adjusted according to the apple butter's thickness)
1½ c. apple butter
1 c. raisins
1 c. pecans, chopped

 Sift together the first four ingredients. Set aside. Beat together the sugar, oil, and eggs. Add apple butter, raisins, and nuts to the wet mixture. Next add the dry ingredients. Mix thoroughly. Pour into two greased 9x5-inch loaf pans. Bake at 375° F. for 50 minutes or until done.

Flag-Flying Birthday Cake

 My friend Joyce Barker prepared a fine birthday dinner for Henry, Sarah, and me when I was expecting David. She served us this fabulous recipe as the untraditional birthday cake. And, why the name "Flag-Flying"? I was born on November 11, which in Virginia is still celebrated as Veteran's Day. When I was a little girl, my Daddy used to point out to me that they flew the flags in our small town "because it is your birthday!"

❧ ❧ ❧ ❧ ❧ ❧

2 c. whole wheat flour
½ tsp. salt
2 tsp. baking soda
¼ c. dry milk powder
¼ c. wheat germ
¾ c. walnuts, ground
1 c. dates, diced
½ c. coconut
½ c. applesauce
2 eggs, beaten
½ c. honey

Combine dry ingredients, then add other things. Pour batter into a greased and floured tube pan. Bake at 350° F. for 35 - 40 minutes. Top with the following glaze:

1/4 c. orange juice
2 tbsp. honey
1 tbsp. butter

Combine the three ingredients in a small saucepan. Boil for 2 or 3 minutes. Pour over cooled cake.

Margot's Apple Strudel

Margot Richter Mayhew, my friend and authority on German food, contributed this recipe, a tempting jelly-roll-like treat. Margot married Roger, an American, and came to this country in 1962 from Huenfeld, Germany.

ತಾತಾತಾ

1 1/3 c. all-purpose flour
1 egg, beaten (Divide in half, reserving part of the beaten egg to brush on the assembled, unbaked strudel.)
1/2 c. milk
1 tbsp. sugar
Dash of salt
Melted butter
Bread crumbs
3 c. apples, thinly sliced
5 tbsp. sugar
2 tbsp. raisins
1 tsp. cinnamon *or* a little lemon juice

Stir together the 1 1/3 c. flour, half an egg, 1/2 c. milk, 1 tbsp. sugar, and salt. Let stand, covered, in a warm place, for 1/2 hour. Then sprinkle some flour on a clean cloth towel and roll out the dough thinly on the towel. Brush the dough liberally with melted butter, and then sprinkle on bread crumbs. Top this with the sliced apples, sugar, raisins, and cinnamon. Use the cloth towel to carefully roll up the entire strudel. Brush it with the remaining egg, and bake on a greased sheet at 350° F. for 45 minutes.

Newlywed Apple Cake

One of the first cakes I baked was this easy entry. I did not know how to make standard frostings, and I did have a 13x9x2-inch pan, so this cake was a good "hands-on-experience" possibility for me. Besides that, the Draper's Meadow Apartment complex in Blacksburg, Virginia, had an ancient, scraggly apple tree near Q-14 (our abode). None of those rough-looking Winesaps went to waste with me around!

☙☙☙☙❧❧❧

$1/2$ c. shortening, butter, *or* margarine
2 c. sugar
2 eggs
2 c. all-purpose flour
1 tsp. cinnamon
1 tsp. nutmeg
1 tsp. baking soda
$1/2$ tsp. salt
4 c. tart apples, sliced
$1/2$ c. pecans *or* walnuts, chopped

Cream together fat, sugar, and eggs. In a separate bowl, sift together dry ingredients. Gradually add to creamed mixture, along with apples and nuts. Pour batter into a greased 13x9x2-inch pan, and bake at 350° F. for 40 minutes.

Meanwhile, make the following topping:

1 c. brown sugar, firmly packed
1 c. water
$1/2$ stick butter *or* margarine

2 tbsp. all-purpose flour
1 tsp. vanilla

Combine all ingredients in a saucepan. Cook slowly until thickened. Spread on hot or cold Newlywed Apple Cake.

Butterscotch Applesauce Cake

When I was a pre-teen and teen, my dermatologist had the notion that chocolate (and about 25 other foods) were to be avoided to prevent and correct acne. (He didn't know then that the zits were hormone-induced!) Therefore, I had to give up my beloved Hershey bars, Baby Ruths, Tootsie Pops, chocolate-covered cherries, and so forth. (Or, at least I was *supposed* to forgo those delights.) Anyway, I happened to also love butterscotch, so eating butterscotch goodies as a substitute for chocolate was not a great sacrifice! Here's a luscious butterscotch-kissed cake.

❧❧❧❦❦❦

½ c. butter *or* margarine
1½ c. sugar
2 eggs
1 tsp. vanilla
2 c. all-purpose flour
1 tsp. baking soda
½ tsp. salt
1 tsp. cinnamon
½ tsp. cloves
1 c. applesauce
⅔ c. butterscotch pieces

Cream butter and sugar; add eggs and vanilla. Beat well. Sift together dry things. Add applesauce alternately with dry ingredients to the creamed mixture. Fold in butterscotch pieces. Pour batter into a greased and floured 13x9x2-inch pan. Bake at 350° F. for 30 minutes or until done.

Meanwhile, prepare the following topping:

2 tbsp. butter
1/3 c. brown sugar, firmly packed
3/4 c. walnuts, chopped
1/2 c. coconut
1/4 c. light cream *or* whipping cream
1/3 c. butterscotch pieces

Heat until butterscotch is melted. Spread over warm baked cake; then run under broiler unit in oven for a minute or two or until the topping is bubbly.

Make-Somebody-Happy Applesauce Cake

Many of my dearest memories involve pets. Besides ducks, chickens, fish, birds, rabbits, cats, turtles, and dogs, I eventually bought my long-dreamed-for horse, a 16-hand-high quarter horse called Gunsmoke. I had saved my allowances and money gifts for years to accumulate enough cash for Gunsmoke. Daddy financed the accouterments: stable, fence, saddle, bridle, grooming tools, feed, shoes, maintenance — the expensive part! What joy it was to finally be up on my own horse, pony tail flying (mine *and* Gunsmoke's), my legs pressed against his warm sides, the world at our feet! And how Gunsmoke enjoyed the apples I collected for him from our yard. I still remember looking into his huge brown appreciative eyes as he gently and greedily slobbered an apple from my palm. (Is there anything on earth softer than a horse's muzzle?)

Now, perhaps this cake has nothing in particular to do with horses, but it does contain applesauce, so bake, and make somebody happy.

ชชชชชชช

4 c. all-purpose flour, sifted
4 tsp. baking soda

1 tsp. salt
2 tsp. cinnamon
½ tsp. nutmeg
½ tsp. cloves
2 tbsp. cocoa

1 c. vegetable oil
2 c. sugar
3 c. unsweetened applesauce, heated
½ c. raisins
½ c. walnuts, chopped

Sift together the first seven ingredients. In a large mixing bowl, combine oil and sugar. Beat. Stir in hot applesauce, blending thoroughly. Add dry ingredients, blending well. Stir in raisins and walnuts. Turn batter into two well-greased and floured 9x9x2-inch cake pans. Bake at 400° F. for 15 minutes; then reduce oven temperature to 375° F. and bake about 15 minutes longer. Remove from oven to cool on wire racks for five minutes. Remove from pans. Cool on rack. Fill and frost with caramel frosting.

Caramel Frosting

½ c. butter
1 c. dark brown sugar, firmly packed
¼ tsp. salt
¼ c. (or a little more) milk
2 c. confectioners' sugar

Melt butter in saucepan over low heat. Stir in brown sugar and salt. Bring to a boil over medium heat; boil hard for two minutes, stirring constantly. Remove from heat. Stir in ¼ c. milk. Return pan to heat; bring to a full boil. Remove from heat; cool to lukewarm. Stir confectioners' sugar into mixture; beat until smooth. If frosting is too thick, beat in a little milk.

Country Kitchen Apple Cake

We all like this recipe, a recent addition to my file, because it's not too sweet — the flavor of apples dominates rather than a sugar taste. If you want to embellish it, though, top with ice cream or such.

❧ ❧ ❧ ❦ ❦ ❦ ❦

3 c. whole wheat flour
1 tsp. baking soda
½ tsp. salt
2 tsp. cinnamon
⅓ - ½ c. sugar
2 eggs, beaten
2 tsp. vanilla
4 c. apples, chopped
1 c. nuts, chopped
1½ c. milk
⅓ c. vegetable oil
⅓ c. honey

Combine the first five ingredients. In a separate bowl, mix the remaining ingredients. Combine the mixtures. Spoon into a well-greased 13x9x2-inch Pyrex dish (or one approximately that size). Bake at 325° F. - 350° F. for 35 minutes, or until a toothpick inserted in the center comes out unsticky.

Old Virginia Applesauce Cake

This next recipe also calls for applesauce, which adds moistness, plus flavor, to baked goods, as do chopped apples. In the old days in New England cider applesauce was made at harvest time. A barrel of it was frozen. (This was before folks had freezers — Mother Nature provided the cold.) As it was needed, chunks of applesauce were cut out and thawed for the table. . . . As Yeats said, however, "Oh, for a beaker full of warm South" where frigid temperatures are seldom felt for very long, and frozen cider applesauce would probably have thawed out fast.

❧❧❧❧❦❦❦

1½ c. applesauce
½ c. shortening
2 c. sugar
1 egg, beaten
2½ c. all-purpose flour
¼ tsp. salt
½ tsp. cinnamon
½ tsp. cloves
½ tsp. allspice
1 c. raisins
½ c. black walnuts, chopped
2 tsp. baking soda
½ c. boiling water

Cream shortening, and add sugar gradually. Add beaten egg and applesauce. Sift flour before measuring. Use a little of the flour to sift over nuts and raisins. Sift remaining flour with salt and spices. Dissolve soda in boiling water. Then add flour mixture alternately with water to creamed sugar and shortening. Then add floured raisins and nuts. Bake in greased tube pan for one hour at 350° F.

Eureka Apple Butter Cake

I looked for a recipe like this for a long time because when we first got married I used to bake a similar cake, but had lost the recipe. What fun to recently come across this old-timey apple butter cake "receipt." Incidentally, since I think apple butter is tops, I used to top my apple butter cake with (you guessed it!) apple butter! Try it on this one.

❧❧❧❧❦❦❦

1½ c. raisins
½ c. water
½ c. butter, at room temperature
2 c. brown sugar
3 eggs, beaten
2 tsp. baking soda, dissolved in 1 tsp. warm water
2 c. apple butter, slightly warmed
3½ c. all-purpose flour
½ tsp. ground cloves
½ tsp. ground nutmeg
1 tsp. cinnamon
1 c. nuts, chopped

In a small saucepan, simmer the raisins and water together for 15 minutes. Cool, drain, and set aside. Cream together butter and brown sugar. Add beaten eggs, soda dissolved in water, and the warm apple butter.

Meanwhile, sift together flour, cloves, nutmeg, and cinnamon. Reserve ¼ c. of this mixture.

Stir the raisins into the butter/apple butter mixture, and add the dry ingredients (except for the ¼ c.). Mix this ¼ c. flour mixture with the nuts, and add to batter. Turn into a greased and floured 10-inch tube pan. Bake at 325° F. for 1½ hours. (This cake freezes well.)

Back to the subject of Johnny Appleseed . . . no doubt he and his contemporaries would be amazed by modern society. Imagine how unbelievable the structure, lighting, equipment, and stock of a present-day supermarket would be to that man of even more simple ways than his peers! — Why, he would not even be allowed to enter a Winn-Dixie (or whatever) because shoes are required, and Johnny Appleseed usually went barefoot. Sometimes when the snow was deep, it is said that he might be seen wearing footgear — perhaps one cast-off moccasin and one old boot. He was not bothered by the cold, nor afraid of snakes in comfortable weather . . . .

A man with a sense of humor, Johnny Appleseed would delight in the wit of this poem, though he might not agree with the sentiments therein. — After the verse is a recipe which, of course, uses premium, clean, smooth, sanitary dried apples!

Dried Apple Pies

I loathe, abhor, detest, despise,
Abominate dried apple pies.
I like good bread, I like good meat,
Or anything that's fit to eat.
But of all the poor grub beneath the skies,
The poorest is dried apple pies.
Give me the toothache, or sore eyes,
But don't give me dried apple pies.
The farmer takes his gnarliest fruit,
'Tis wormy, bitter and hard to boot.
He leaves the hulls to make us cough,
And don't take half the peeling off.
Then on a dirty cord 'tis strung
And in a garret window hung,
And there it serves as roost for flies,
Until it's made up into pies.
Tread on my corns, or tell me lies,
But don't pass me dried apple pies.

– Author Unknown

Dried Apple Cake

2 c. dried apples
2 c. molasses
1 c. raisins
1 c. butter
1 c. buttermilk *or* sour milk
1 c. brown sugar

2 eggs, well-beaten
1½ tsp. baking soda
2 tsp. cinnamon
½ tsp. cloves
½ tsp. nutmeg
3 c. all-purpose flour

Soak dried apples 10 hours in cold water. Drain and chop finely; cook slowly with molasses 1 hour. Add raisins. Stir well. Cool. Cream butter, gradually adding sugar, eggs, cooled mixture, buttermilk or sour milk, and flour mixed and sifted with soda and spices. Turn into a well-buttered tube or Bundt pan and bake until done (60 - 75 minutes) at 350° F.

Midwest Apple Pie Cake

You will like this dessert, which is, as the name denotes, sort of a cross between cake and pie.

❦❦❦❦❦❦

½ c. butter, melted
1 tsp. baking soda
1 tbsp. cinnamon
2½ c. apples, diced
2 tbsp. boiling water
1 tsp. salt (or less to taste)
¼ c. walnuts, finely chopped
1 c. sugar
1 c. all-purpose flour
1 egg, beaten

Combine in order. Pour into a 9-inch greased pie pan. Bake at 350° F. for 40 minutes. Cut in wedges. Top with whipped cream or ice cream.

Mama's Apple Pie

I like my mother's apple pie better than any other I have ever eaten. Hers is not too buttery (that "greasy" taste of too much fat ruins the fresh taste of the apples in many apple pie recipes). It has the perfect balance of cinnamon and sugar (not too heavy or pronounced like some). She makes an excellent crust — the proper thickness and texture (see the next recipe). She uses a heart-shaped cookie cutter to make darling-looking vents for the steam to escape. She flutes the edges attractively. She uses fresh apples (no canned apple pie filling allowed). Mama's Apple Pie is the quintessential, honest, simple, classic, way-it-should-be apple pie!

5 c. tart apples
$3/4$ c. sugar
2 tbsp. all-purpose flour
Dash of salt
$1 1/2$ tsp. cinnamon
2 tbsp. butter
Unbaked double pie crust

Put sliced apples in pastry shell. Mix sugar, flour, salt, and cinnamon. Sprinkle over apples. Dot with butter. Adjust top crust, flute pastry edge, and make air vents. Bake at 350° F. for an hour.

Unsurpassed Pie Pastry

For a 9-inch double-crust pie:

$2 1/2$ c. all-purpose flour
1 tsp. salt
$3/4$ c. shortening
5 - 6 tbsp. very cold water

Sift together the flour and salt; cut in the shortening until the mixture is in particles the size of small peas. Add the water, one tablespoon at a time, stirring to form a ball. Separate the dough into two balls. Chill. Roll out onto a lightly-floured surface. Place one crust in the pie pan. Add apple filling (other fillings can also be used, of course). Put on top crust. Trim and flute edge. Prick with a fork to allow air to escape; or make air vents with a cookie cutter, as my mother does.

Crazy Crust Apple Pie

Remember when crazy crust recipes came on the scene in the early 1970's? They were quite a hit! I suppose the two most popular (with me, at least) were Crazy Crust Pizza and Crazy Crust Apple Pie. It's time to revive such convenient, tasty recipes! Here's the apple one.

֍֍֍֍֍֍

1 c. all-purpose flour
1 tsp. baking powder
$1/2$ tsp. salt
2 tbsp. sugar
1 egg
$2/3$ c. shortening
$3/4$ c. water

1 (21-oz.) can apple pie filling
1 tbsp. lemon juice
$1/2$ tsp. cinnamon

Combine the first seven ingredients. Mix at least 2 minutes with an electric mixer. Pour into a greased 9-inch pie pan. Next, mix the remaining three ingredients. Pour into the center of the batter. Do not stir! Bake at 425° F. for about 45 minutes.

By the way, my friend and cooking corespondent, recipe collector Peggy Cook of Knoxville, Tennessee, reminded me of *"an old apple favorite." Here are her words: "Mother [they lived in Tennessee] made fried apple pies which as a child I loved — more so than a pie — one could hold the little half moon pies in the hand and walk around eating them . . . they are not made as often today . . . ."*

Whispering Pines Fruit Kuchen

Susan Holzwart of Whispering Pines Orchard in Cleveland, Wisconsin, contributed the following recipe. Sliced apples, peaches, or the fruit of your choice can be used in this irresistible dessert.

ૡૡૡૡૡૡૡ

$1\frac{1}{2}$ c. all-purpose flour
$\frac{3}{4}$ c. butter
$\frac{1}{2}$ tsp. salt
1 egg, beaten
2 tbsp. milk
3 c. fruit, sliced
3 eggs, beaten
$1 - 1\frac{1}{2}$ c. sugar
2 tbsp. all-purpose flour
$\frac{3}{4}$ c. milk
$\frac{1}{2}$ c. sugar
2 tbsp. butter, softened
$\frac{1}{2}$ c. all-purpose flour

To assemble this dish, first cut together the $1\frac{1}{2}$ c. flour, $\frac{3}{4}$ c. butter, and $\frac{1}{2}$ tsp. salt until the mixture resembles coarse meal. Add 1 beaten egg and 2 tbsp. milk, stirring well. Press this dough into the bottom and sides of an ungreased 9x13x2-inch pan. Put the 3 c. sliced (or chopped) apples or whatever on top.

Next make a custard by mixing together 3 eggs, $1 - 1\frac{1}{2}$ c. sugar, 2 tbsp. flour, and $\frac{3}{4}$ c. milk. Pour this over the fruit in the pan.

Finally, make the topping by combining ½ c. sugar, 2 tbsp. soft butter, and ½ c. flour. Cut these ingredients together (using a fork or two small knives), forming a creamy/crumbly mixture. Pat this topping over the ingredients in the pan.

Bake at 350° F. for 40 minutes or until the fruit is tender.

Applestreuselkuchen

Following is another recipe from my German friend, Margot Richter Mayhew.

ৰু ৰু ৰু ৰু ৰু ৰু

3 c. all-purpose flour
1 tbsp. baking yeast
4 tbsp. sugar
1 tsp. salt
A few drops of lemon juice, *or* a small amount of grated lemon
   peel
1 c. lukewarm milk
¼ c. shortening

Put a little of the flour (about ¼ c.), the yeast, ½ c. of the milk, and 1 tsp. sugar in a bowl. Stir together, cover with a cloth, and let rise in a warm place. Add the remaining ingredients. Knead until smooth and elastic. Roll out on a greased cookie sheet to a ½ inch-thickness. Let rise, covered, in a warm place, until doubled in bulk.

Cover the dough with thin slices of apples in neat rows, close together.

Make a **crumb topping** by cutting together:

1 c. all-purpose flour
¾ c. sugar

1 tsp. cinnamon
1 stick butter

Sprinkle this crumbly mixture over the top of the apples. Bake at 400° F. for 20 - 30 minutes.

Dutch Apple Pie

4 c. apples
1 (9-inch) unbaked pastry shell
2 tbsp. flour (all-purpose, unbleached, *or* whole wheat)
3/4 c. sugar
Dash of salt
1 tsp. cinnamon
1 tbsp. lemon juice, if apples are not tart

Slice apples (they do not need to be peeled) into an unbaked pastry shell, and sprinkle the mixture of flour, sugar, salt, and cinnamon over the apples. Add lemon juice if desired. Top with:

2/3 c. flour (all-purpose, unbleached, *or* whole wheat)
1/3 c. brown sugar, firmly packed
1/3 c. butter, softened

Blend the flour, brown sugar, and butter together, and pat over the pie. Bake at 350° F. for about 40 minutes.

Speaking again of John Chapman, he was regarded as a holy person, a "medicine man" among the Indians. Johnny had once met a Native American sick with fever. Using his knowledge of medicinal plants, combined, I'm sure, with Christian prayer, Johnny was able to effect a cure. That action was the beginning of friendship between the Indians and the orchardman.

However, during the strange War of 1812 (in that conflict neither the United States nor England gained one inch of territory, yet the war cost $100 million, 1,400 ships, and 51,000 men, and the eventual peace treaty did not even mention the original cause of the war), in which the Indians sided with the British, Johnny was put in the position of frontier messenger. In that role the gentle, peace-loving man became a military hero credited with saving the fort at Mansfield, Ohio.

The way it happened was this: though Johnny refused to fight the Indians, he felt duty-bound to help the white settlers. When he heard that the Indians had an attack planned, Johnny hurried through the wilderness advising pioneers to flee to the safety of the Madison fort blockhouses and cannon. The people complied, but soon the fort was over-filled. There was not enough food, and the spring (for water) was outside the walls of the fort. The settlers were trapped, with the Indians lurking in the surrounding woods. The remaining hope was intervention from the military garrison at Mount Vernon, thirty miles away. Only one courageous person volunteered to go for help: Johnny Appleseed asked to go, facing the threat of death at the hands of the Indians. He made the journey on foot, stealthily traversing the forest, walking all night. When he reached Mount Vernon, he gave the message, and then led the soldiers back toward Mansfield. Just before reaching the fort he stopped to sleep in a log. The soldiers arrived in time to repel a Shawnee attack already underway. John Chapman had saved the day!

It is said that after his heroic act (and a snooze), Johnny Appleseed awakened to tend an orchard in need of work near Madison. Never forgetting his priorities of spreading apple trees and the Gospel, eventually Johnny Appleseed looked to less-settled areas west of Ohio. In the 1830's, he left Ohio and roamed the lands of Indiana, Wisconsin, Michigan, Iowa, and Illinois.

The following recipe, from the March, 1893 issue of ***The Delineator*** *magazine, seems to fit well in a book commemorating apples and Johnny Appleseed.*

Apple Johnny-Cake

This is an old-fashioned New England supper dish, but is equally attractive for breakfast or luncheon. Mix a pint of corn-meal with a scanty half-cupful of sugar, a pinch of salt and a teaspoonful of cream of tartar. Dissolve half a teaspoonful of soda in a little milk, and stir it into the meal with more milk, mixing thoroughly until a dough as thick as pancake batter is produced. Then add to the dough three thinly-sliced sour or sweet apples, and bake for thirty-five minutes if the apples are sour, or fifty if they are sweet. The oven should not be very hot. A wide pan should be used in baking, that the cake may be thin and be thoroughly cooked throughout. If the crust seems likely to become too thick, set the pan upon a trivet and cover the cake with brown paper.

The next two recipes demonstrate the use of apples, first in combination with pears and then with pumpkin. Incidentally, old-timers recall "apple-slump, apple-mose, apple crowdy, apple-tarts, mess apple-pies, and puff apple-pies." In 1758, Dr. Israel Acrelius, a Swedish parson, wrote about such foods in Delaware:

"Apple-pie is used through the whole year, and when fresh apples are no longer to be had, dried ones are used. It is the evening meal of children. House-pie, in country places, is made of apples neither peeled nor freed from their cores, and its crust is not broken if a wagon wheel goes over it."

– from Alice Morse Earle, **Home Life in Colonial Days***, The Macmillan Company, New York, 1898, p. 146.*

Apple-Pear Pie

Unbaked pie pastry, for 9-inch, 2-crust pie
3 medium apples, peeled, cored, and sliced

2 good-sized pears, peeled, cored, and sliced
1 tsp. apple pie spice
$2/3$ c. sugar (or less if fruit is sweet)
2 tbsp. brown sugar
2 tbsp. butter *or* margarine

Mix fruit and apple pie spice. Place the fruit in the pie shell, and add sugar into which the butter has been cut. Add top crust. Flute edge and make slits for steam to escape. Bake at 400° F. for 30 - 40 minutes or until the fruit is tender, and the crust lightly browned.

Pioneer Pumpkin – Apple Butter Pie

1 c. mashed, cooked pumpkin
1 c. apple butter
1 (14-oz.) can condensed milk
2 eggs, beaten
$1/2$ tsp. cinnamon
$1/4$ tsp. *each* of salt, ginger, and nutmeg
1 unbaked (9-inch) pie shell
Whipped cream, if desired

In a mixing bowl, combine the pie filling ingredients and mix well. Pour into the pie shell. Bake at 425° F. for 15 minutes, then reduce heat to 350° F. Bake for 35 minutes more, checking to be sure that the crust does not get overly brown. Cool on a wire rack. Serve plain or topped with whipped cream.

Long before Johnny Appleseed embarked on his life's mission, apple tree production was encouraged by other forward-thinking Americans. John Endicott and John Winthrop, first and second governors of the Massachusetts Bay Colony, are variously credited with bringing the first English apple saplings to America. As early as 1629, Massachusetts colonists were urged to plant English apple seeds in New World soil.

The early colonists had, of course, found wild apple trees growing here, but the fruit was described as being hard, small, acid-tasting; too tart and sour. However, by 1700, cultivated trees were producing well. Rhode Island Greenings were being successfully grown in and around Newport, Rhode Island. This variety was considered an excellent pie apple. Other orchards, too, were producing desirable apples, and by 1741, New England was even exporting apples to the West Indies. Nowadays, there are over 7,000 varieties of apples grown in the U.S. (and 3,000 additional varieties grown elsewhere).

*Surprisingly, the first cookbook published in this country (**American Cookery**, by Amelia Simmons, 1796) contained a recipe for an apple pie made with applesauce, rather than with sliced apples. Here is a modern version of this concept.*

Applesauce Pies

2 unbaked (9-inch) pie shells
1 (1-lb.) can applesauce
3 eggs, beaten
1 tsp. vanilla
1 c. sugar
$1/8$ tsp. salt
$1/2$ tsp. cinnamon
1 stick butter *or* margarine, melted

Combine the above ingredients and pour into two pie shells. Bake at 325° F. for 30 - 40 minutes.

Heirloom Apple Fritters

In New Orleans, fritters are called beignets, their French name. And what a joy are those airy puffs sprinkled with confectioners' sugar! Husband Henry and I have indulged in our share of those treats. We have also eaten tasty conch fritters in

Nassau! But, one of my most vivid "fritter memories" involves sitting beside a mammoth blazing fireplace at the Peerless Mill Inn near Dayton, Ohio. As the flames danced and crackled, Henry and I feasted on roast duckling accompanied by (among other things) sweet potato fritters. . . . Hmm, I wonder if Johnny Appleseed ever set foot on that particular acre of Ohio?

಄಄಄಄಄಄಄

1 c. all-purpose flour
1 tsp. baking powder
$1/2$ tsp. salt
2 tbsp. sugar
1 egg
$1/3$ c. milk
1 c. apple, finely chopped
Vegetable oil
Confectioners' sugar

Combine dry ingredients. Add liquids; beat until smooth and then blend in apples. Drop by teaspoons into 375° F. hot oil. Cook until lightly browned; turn and brown other side. Remove and drain on paper towels. Roll in confectioners' sugar and serve.

Extraordinarily Good Apple Butter Bars

When I took a batch of these out-of-this-world cookies to a church Christmas party, Seif Hussamy immediately asked for my recipe. He explained that his Syrian mother used to bake a date-type cookie which he loved, that tasted like these. His mom always shooed him out of the kitchen (only the girls were supposed to learn the family cooking secrets), so he never solved this culinary mystery. Others at the party also raved over the cookies and variously guessed their identity. — Figs? Dates? What? No one suspected *apple butter*!

These cookies are worth "sacrificing" the apple butter for. (Most homemakers tend to dole out such delicacies as good preserves, jellies, pickles, and the like.) Go ahead and splurge, and if you want to save that jar of homemade apple butter you can use the grocery-store kind for this recipe!

ೀೀೀೀೀೀ

1 c. whole wheat flour
$1/2$ c. brown sugar, firmly packed
6 tbsp. butter or margarine, softened at room temperature
$3/4$ c. apple butter
1 c. quick oats
$1/2$ c. pecans, chopped
1 tsp. lemon rind, grated

Combine flour and sugar. Cut in butter until the mixture resembles coarse crumbs. Mix in oats. Grease an 8-inch square pan and press $1 3/4$ c. of this crumbly mixture into the pan. Stir together apple butter, nuts, and lemon rind. Spread this apple butter mixture on top of the oat mixture in the pan to within half an inch of the edges. Sprinkle on remaining oat mixture, and press down with the palm of the hand firmly but carefully. Bake at 350° F. for about 35 minutes or until the edges begin to brown slightly. Cool in the pan on a wire rack. To serve, cut into 16 squares.

Winter Thaw Hot Cider

Early Americans were refreshed by sweet cider (apple juice), and made merry by hard (fermented cider). Cider is superb served plain, or fancy like this.

5 c. apple cider
$1/4$ c. lemon juice

2 - 4 tbsp. brown sugar
4 whole cloves
1 cinnamon stick, broken
½ tsp. ground ginger
1 tsp. vanilla

Heat together everything (except the vanilla) for 10 minutes. Add vanilla, stir, and serve.

On-the-Wagon Champagne

To conclude this book, let's drink a non-alcoholic toast to Johnny Appleseed and all the other industrious men and women who have grown apples and developed recipes for using the fruit!

☙☙☙❧❧❧❧

Combine equal parts of apple cider and ginger ale. Bubbly and refreshing!

A votre santé — to your health!